SEASONS OF THE HEART

—— one year of poems ——

SOPHIA MORRIS

WESTBOW
PRESS®
A DIVISION OF THOMAS NELSON
& ZONDERVAN

WestBow Press books may be ordered through
booksellers or by contacting:

WestBow Press
A Division of Thomas Nelson & Zondervan
1663 Liberty Drive
Bloomington, IN 47403
www.westbowpress.com
844-714-3454

ISBN: 979-8-3850-2086-7 (sc)
ISBN: 979-8-3850-2087-4 (e)

Library of Congress Control Number: 2024904828

Print information available on the last page.

WestBow Press rev. date: 06/26/2024

To those who are brokenhearted
and in need of healing…
God sees you, he hears you, and he loves you.
More than you will ever know.

It does get better. Trust me.
I'm cheering you on.

"There is a time for everything,
and a season for every activity under the heavens:
a time to be born and a time to die,
a time to plant and a time to uproot,
a time to kill and a time to heal,
a time to tear down and a time to build,
a time to weep and a time to laugh,
a time to mourn and a time to dance,
a time to scatter stones and a time to gather them,
a time to embrace and a time to
refrain from embracing,
a time to search and a time to give up,
a time to keep and a time to throw away,
a time to tear and a time to mend,
a time to be silent and a time to speak,
a time to love and a time to hate,
a time for war and a time for peace.

He has made everything beautiful in its time.
He has also set eternity in the human heart;
yet no one can fathom what God has
done from beginning to end."

Ecclesiastes 3:1-8, 11

CONTENTS

CONTENTS

INTRODUCTION

Why does God allow hard things to happen to us? Why does heartbreak hurt so much? Why are we scared to be known when we so strongly desire to be loved? Is it really worth it?

You've probably wondered about these things before. I asked myself those questions over and over again during the process of writing and compiling these poems. Though I wish I could say I found all the answers, I believe that I'm a few steps closer to answering those big "why" questions.

This book chronicles the journey of searching. It tells the story of love, loss, hope, and healing. It is deep and vulnerable, exciting and emotional.

And these poems were all written within one year.

It has taken me much longer to publish this book, though. It's scary to share a piece of your heart with others. But I have decided that if these poems bring someone one step closer to Jesus, then it's all worth it. All the tears I cried, all the pain I felt, all the time I spent writing, all the fears I had to conquer to publish this…if it brings one person closer to the heart of God, then it's all worth it.

A friend asked me recently what I would say to the younger version of myself that wrote these poems. My response was this:

"Be patient with yourself.
God is writing a good story."

And that's my desire for you in sharing this book. I hope you find yourself in these poems. Not only that, but I pray you find Jesus. I found him in the midst of my deepest pain. Looking back, I realized that Jesus was with me all along.

The same is true for you. Jesus sits alongside you—sometimes weeping with you, sometimes wiping the tears from your eyes, and sometimes simply holding you in his arms. I hope you find some encouragement in that truth.

You are seen.
You are known.
You are loved.
You are never alone.

Healing is possible, and it's not too far away.
I'm cheering you on :)

QUIET

I have a quiet heart
Don't want a lot
Just a hand to hold
And a heart to love

I have a quiet voice
Listen more than I speak
But I'm not shy
Just thinking

I have a quiet love
Scared to say it out loud
Worried if you knew my thoughts
You'd walk away

This is a quiet space
The room between us
Too far to reach sometimes
Do you notice the space?

I don't think you understand
I would be happy with you
Anywhere at all
Just quietly walking

But when I'm really with you
I can't help myself
I want to know everything
So I ask a million questions

And then I listen
I memorize the details
What you said, how you said it
And how it made me feel

What you wore, where you sat
What were you looking at?
I remember all the things
You spoke through the quiet

The silence is easy to misinterpret
So that's why I dream
To fill the quiet space
With lovely little things

Memories that never happened
One-way conversations
Thinking of everything
But the quiet reality

It's here now
Right in front of my face
The words I could read
But would never speak

So please, help me out
I want to hear your words
Speak across the quiet space
Do you think you could love me?

DRY LIGHTNING

Dry lighting
Nature's crescendo
As light slices through the night
Tearing the sky apart
The black curtain broken

The toasted air
Clouds but no rain
No pitter patter
But the tap tap tap of my feet
Sneaking across dry pavement

It's dark
It's late
It's eerie
But I'm safe

Flashes of light
Illuminate my eyes
And I am intrigued
Intrigued and in awe
Such a strange night

My heart is full of
Dry lightning
Fire and passion
Sharp and bright
A lonely companion
For this empty night

Dry lightning
Strikes again
I've lost count
How many times?
Is it close?
Has it come for me yet?

Nope.
Not yet.
Keep waiting.

It's only dry lightning

PATIENCE, SWEET GIRL

Patience, sweet girl
As you wait for someday
These moments are precious
You can change the world on your way

A lifetime of love
Isn't built in a day
Patience, sweet girl
Today is not someday

I know it's hard
It's really hard to wait
But the waiting makes it sweeter
When you get to someday

But what if someday
Never comes?
What if a man never decides
It's me he loves?

God, give me the courage
God, give me the strength
To say not my will,
But I want it your way

Renew my dreams
Brush the tears off my cheek
Yes, today is Monday
But that means it's a new week

Walk around
With your head held high
Look up and appreciate
The bright blue sky

Rejoice in knowing
That God is writing every letter
And your story doesn't end here
It's gonna get better

Close your eyes
Breathe in, breathe out
Be still and know
That even in the doubts

God is good
He is fighting for you
He has a plan
Even if it's not what you'd choose

Yes, this is hard
I know your heart hurts
But I know this God
And I know he's writing sweet words

STARS

Look up
Look up in the night sky
See the stars?
I see them too

They connect us
A beautiful reminder
Of the light above
That watches over us

You and me
Together or apart
Makes no difference to the light
It will shine just the same

Side by side
Or a million miles away
Light is still up there
Winking back at us

So trust that there is light
But don't trust in the stars
Trust the one who placed them there
He knows each one by name

He knows you, too
He knows your name
He knows your scars
He knows your heart

He knows where you've fallen
And all those times you refused to give up
Always fighting
Fighting for light

So trust
Trust that he has a plan
His plans are good
And one day, you'll see the beauty in it all

All the stars
And all the sky
All the light
And all the night

Even darkness has a purpose
It allows the light to shine
The stars will remain
When morning takes their place

The day that comes
Hides their light
Yet as the sun sets
And night arrives

Those same stars come out to greet us
So look up in the beautiful night sky
Trust in the one who made the stars
And the one who placed them there

He made your heart, too
He has a purpose and a plan
And he makes it all beautiful
According to heavenly time

Just wait for night to come
And you'll see how light shines
A gentle reminder of all his goodness
Winking back at us

ICED SUNSET

You know that feeling when the sun is bright
But you're still so cold?
When the sunset is beautiful
But you feel the wind in your bones?

Do you ever get the feeling
That everything is bright
But what you sense inside
Tells you something's not right?

What is it about beauty
That makes us think of all we lack?
Sometimes when I'm the most grateful
Is when I feel the most sad

Why does the wind blow cold
On a warm summer day?
Why does it have to ruin perfection
In such a cruel way?

Why is the beach always colder?
Is it just not what I expect?
If I expect perfection,
The opposite is what I get

Maybe this is hard
Because I imagined a fantasy
A world that doesn't exist
Is the only one I want to see

Maybe it's time I started daydreaming
Of something more practical

Instead of daisies and butterflies
I'll remember the sunset cold

Maybe light can still shine
Even if I don't feel its warmth
Maybe God is still good
Even in the storm

Maybe the storm is surprising
Because we didn't expect it
All the while, he was sleeping
And we just didn't get it

God didn't promise clear skies
He didn't promise gentle waves
He didn't promise a perfect sunset
So why do we expect life that way?

It's good to look for beauty
It's good to have faith
It's good to expect God to move
But it always comes his way

Maybe he planned the storm
And maybe he planned his nap
So that when the storm scares us,
On his shoulder we would tap

A cold sunset reminds me
It's time to bundle up
Just as the waves remind me
Only Jesus is enough

UNWRITTEN HISTORY

I'm not sure what I'm supposed to do
When I have to walk around without you

Do I need to give you space?
Or can we be in the same place?

I thought I was hiding it well
But it seems like everyone can tell

Why does everyone else see
That there's something of a we?

Everyone and their mother
Seems to think we're together

But you assure them that we're friends
Which means someone has a broken lens

Are you really so blind?
Or is it all in my mind?

Maybe you see it too
And you just don't want me with you

That brings us back to the present
I'm not sure where my mind went

I can't seem to figure out
Which way is the best route

I don't want to stay away
When everything is gray

I almost wish it was black or white
So I could let you out of my sight

But I think that would kill me
You see, it's tricky

When I see you, it hurts
But when I don't, it's worse

I know that you're not mine
But I'll stay around if that's fine

It's my heart that keeps me here
And it keeps my mind unclear

Is it too late to say hello?
Do I have to let you go?

Because if I happen to say hi
Then I'll have to say goodbye

I still don't know
Which way to go

I feel silly this way
Like a lovesick cliche

It's all in reverse
And I don't know which is worse

So for now, we're still a mystery
Just pieces of unwritten history

WITNESS TO LOVE

If comparison is the thief of joy
Right now it's a high speed chase
I'm sprinting down the highway
With you setting the pace

I tell myself to stop running
It's not worth it, he's not the one
But some days I believe the lie
That if it's not you, it's no one

I didn't even get the chance
To love you the way I wanted to
But if there was never a with
How can there be a without you?

I tell myself again and again
Maybe it's better this way
But am I sure it is?
I don't know what to say

I'm anxious and confused
I'm angry and I'm sad
All these emotions in my head
And it's all just my bad

I'm sorry for wasting your time
I'm sorry for making a mess
I'm sorry for trying to love you
I'm sorry, I did my best

And it's okay if that's not what you want
I just wish I knew before
To save myself from this
And to wait for what's in store

I'll get out of your way now
I'll try to move along
I'll write some sad poetry
And listen to sad songs

And slowly, I will heal
And slowly, I will grow
As I learn that sometimes
Even a smile can say no

For now, I'm just a witness
As I stare at the crime scene
I'll leave the stolen car
But keep the memories

This high-speed chase
Has come to an end
And this broken road
Will begin to mend

At least now we know
Even if it hurts a little
The verdict of the case
Is love's acquittal

You're free to go
You're not to blame
Don't worry now
I've cleared your name

It's my turn next
What will the verdict be?
The judge holds the gavel
As I give my testimony

One day, one day
I hope I'll understand
For now I'll walk on boldly
And take the witness stand

SAND ON THE BEACH

I used to dream of warm sunsets
And long walks on the beach
With salt in our hair
And sand beneath our feet

I still have this dream
But with a slightly different view
Sometimes I'm alone, sometimes I'm not
But I'm no longer walking with you

I can't forget all the memories we made
But now, when I look back, I see
That the sand on the beach
Was just sand in an hourglass

The waves come to shore
And wash the light away
As I realize it's not tomorrow
And the answer is no today

As the sunset fades into night
The sand beneath my feet grows cold
And that dreamy summer day
Remains a story yet untold

I stand on the shore
Of a sinking beach
Wondering if the sky above
Will always be too far to reach

I've emptied my tears into
An ocean with no drought
Now I'm healing, slowly
Just waiting for time to run out

LAST WITHOUT A FIRST

This is the last time.
The last time I hold you.
The last time I love you.
Not that there was a first.

Oops, I did it again.
I loved and I loved and
I let my heart get away and
I got nothing in return.

I said I was done with this.
That I wouldn't let it happen again.
I tried to avoid regret
And yet here we are again.

But this time, it feels different.
This time, it was supposed to work out.
This time, he was supposed to be the one.
Or at least SOMEone.

But who am I to think
That any of this would work out?
That my life would go according to my plan?
That I had God's plans figured out?

But oh well.
I can't go back now.
The past is in the past.
No turning back.

So here I am, saying my last goodbye.
Saying those sweet words for the last time.
Saying what I wish I'd said earlier
But never got the chance to.

Saying for the last time,
I love you.

Not that there was a first.

MOVING ON

My heart hurts and I don't even know why
My head hurts from trying to figure it out
My soul aches and I think I need to cry
But I think maybe I should move on

How long is too long
For me to dwell on this?
When does a love song
Become a felony?

Have my feelings changed
Or is this more of the same?
I go back and forth
Like this is some silly game

Is that all this is to you?
Do you think it's funny?
If you're truly not desperate
Then why do you keep running?

I refuse to believe
That you enjoy this race
It looks exhausting
To try to keep that pace

You open one door
And sprint to the next
Like a salesman on the clock
With a quota to make

Okay, so I was wrong
Could I ever be right?
If you don't love me now
Do you think someday you might?

I want to hold my heart in suspense
Waiting just in case
You change your mind
And give up the chase

But I'm done
I can't do this anymore
I have to stop
Stop waiting at the door

Goodbye for now
This is the hardest part
God, give me the courage to say
Goodbye from the bottom of my heart

SHIPWRECK

We used to be ships
Sailing across the sea
With the wind in our sails
And deep blue water beneath

That ship has sailed
That voyage is done
There was no anchor to keep
That ship from being sunk

Down, down, down
Drowning in the salty sea
Waves thundering above
Pounding it to smithereens

I look back on those days
When we sailed atop clear waters
Shaking my head in shame
Saying of course it didn't last longer

I should've known all along
Our ship was meant to sink
It didn't crash, just fell apart
Taking on water silently

I don't think you ever noticed
That this ship never anchored
A fact that makes me mildly sad
Where I could've been angered

You made it safe to shore
You're exploring new places now
While I look for another island
I keep coming back somehow

Back to the ship's graveyard
Where my foolish dream was laid to rest
I know I can't fix a sunken ship
But for some reason, I can't resist

I keep diving deep underwater
As the pressure in my ears builds
And each time I swim back to the shipwreck
I feel a weird sense of guilt

I feel like I'm doing something wrong
Like I shouldn't keep coming back here
Scared someone will call me insane
When I'm just looking for something familiar

Familiarity, that's what the shipwreck brings
Even if all hope is lost
There's still a piece of my heart
Buried beneath the waves tossed

HEY, FRIEND

Hey, friend
I just wanted to say
I know it's been hard
But you'll be okay

You're doing your best
That's all you can do
The fate of the world
Is not up to you

I can see the pain
Weighing you down
As you cry silently
Not making a sound

I see you there
You're not alone
You don't have to do this
On your own

It's okay to admit
You don't have it all together
And that you need help
Fighting against the weather

I see the storm inside
No, you're not the only one
Who feels like this sometimes
Like you want to hide or run

What you feel, it's okay
You don't have to hide from me
I'll sit here with you
And listen to the sea

As the waves crash
On shifting sand
Uncertainty lies
In not knowing where to stand

You're not expected
To have it all figured out
So next time it's confusing,
Don't jump into doubt

Maybe it's okay to pause
Maybe it's okay to not know
Maybe it's okay to wait
And take this slow

Each day the sun rises
Is another reminder
To give yourself grace
And learn to be kinder

You're not perfect
And that's okay
I wouldn't want it
Any other way

That's what makes us human
The fact that we fall
This life is a journey
That's the best part of all

You're okay, friend
Things will get better
In the meantime,
Let's do this together

SO MUCH LOVE

Sometimes I ask God,
"Why would you let me love him so much?"

I know this is all part of a bigger plan
But right now, that plan doesn't feel good

And God, I know that this world
Doesn't revolve around my feelings

But sometimes it just hurts a lot
And I wish I had a logical explanation

So I will be still
And wait for you to speak

Trusting that even in the silence
You are good to me

God only knows
What all this is for

But God only knows
What's behind that closed door

God only knows
What else he saved me from

But I know enough to know
That I don't want to run

I'll stay by his side
And wait for the light

Trusting that each new day
Brings a new fight

And every battle I find myself in
Is another opportunity to let God win

I surrender it all
God, I'll let you move

If it's shaking the mountains
Or breaking my heart

Whatever it takes,
Just bring me close to you

God, I want to know more of who you are
The only thing I want to chase is your heart

I don't have the answers to all my questions
But I'll keep asking them just the same

Knowing that his plans are good
Even when they're not safe

I trust you, God
I will wait patiently

I trust you, God
I want your will, your way

As I reflect on your faithfulness
Despite all that I've done

I will ask you one more question:
"God, how could you love me so much?"

EVERYTHING

You placed the stars up in the sky
You raised the mountains way up high

You placed the ground under my feet
You listen to every heartbeat

You paint the colors of a sunset
You know the hairs on my head

You dug the depths of the ocean
You give freedom to emotion

You speak truth through a whisper
You shake the whole earth with thunder

You set wildfires ablaze
You soften hearts with your gaze

You are solid as a rock
You are graceful as a hawk

You are gentle and kind
You are strong and wise

You are all these things
You are my everything

And still I can't see
Why you choose to love me

I'll never understand
The details of your plan

And I know I cannot earn
This grace I don't deserve

Yet you pour your blessings out
I still don't understand how

How your grace and love for me
Reaches far and wide and deep

It covers all my sin and shame
It takes away the pain and blame

You've washed me clean
In your eyes, I am free

Free to laugh and dance and cry
Free to marvel and wonder why

As I stand in utter awe
Of this beautiful love song

Your words are a melody
That makes my bitter heart sweet

For everything we've been through
All I can say is thank you

Thank you for loving, for choosing,
For seeing, and for proving

That your love for us
Is completely boundless

I could go on and on and on
And still I'd sing an empty song

For I can never do justice
To how much you love us

There are not enough words on a page
Not enough lights on a stage

To honor you the way you deserve
So instead, I promise to serve

Your purpose, your kingdom, your will, your way
I'll let my actions and what I say

Be a chorus that praises your name
And tells the world of your fame

Be the light in me
And let others see

This joy, this peace, this love
Only comes from above

This life I live
Is the good you give

And I am only free
Because of Christ in me

HEALING

I'm healing, slowly
It's taken so long
But I'm happy to say
I'm finally moving on

Healing doesn't always come
With the crash of a wave
Instead, it's found
In the falling rain

As tears stream
Down my face
I feel the pain
Softly melt away

It's amazing how healing comes
From releasing tears
And sharing burdens
And speaking fears

What if I wasn't
Broken after all?
Maybe it just took
A nasty fall

For me to remember
That I can't do this alone
I need a Savior
And someone to lean on

The same God
Who spoke light into being
Is the same God
Who speaks truth over me

The same God
Who calmed the storm
Is the same God
Who calms my heart

The same God
Who holds the world
Is the same God
Who holds my hurt

I'm healing, slowly
And growing, too
A deep breath and
"God, thank you"

SEASONS CHANGE

Seasons change
But some things stay the same

I love you still
And I always will

Thank you for all the lessons
You taught me without knowing

I fell in love, I fell apart, and now
I'm falling to fall back into place

The coldest winter of my life
And the warmest summer night

This year has seen it all
Winter, spring, summer, fall

I had hope
I sang a sweet song

I felt rejection
I had to move on

I embraced the change
While wading through pain

I'm learning to grow
Out of the cold snow

There will be days with pain
There will be days with rain

There will be long, dark nights
There will be days with endless light

But one thing remains
Only one thing is true

Fix your eyes on Jesus
And he'll see you through

He won't always take it away
But he'll always walk with you

He won't always save the day
But he'll always love you

Trust me when I say
That he is enough

God is good
And that is good enough

Even when it makes no sense
He is on the throne

The king reigns forever
Through the rain, the sun, the snow

Seasons change
But one thing stays the same

He loves you still
And he always will

HERE'S TO THE
UNCERTAINTY

So here's to learning to be comfortable
Even amidst the uncertainty

I am learning that I can grow
Even when I don't know what I'm growing towards

There is a time for everything
And a moment for every emotion

A time to grow and a time to prune
A time to work and a time to rest
A time to run and a time to slow down
A time to fight and a time to surrender
A time to wait and a time to dance
A time to laugh and a time to cry
A time to understand and a time to be uncertain

Here's to the moments
When we don't know what we feel
Here's to the times
When we don't feel certain about anything
Here's to the seasons
When our thoughts are as cloudy as the skies

Because there is always time for grace
There is always time for love
There is always time for joy
There is always time for peace
There is always time for hope
There is always time for growth
There is always time to be grateful

So here's to the seasons of uncertainty

Here's to learning how to be comfortable being uncomfortable

Here's to the unknown

Printed in the United States
by Baker & Taylor Publisher Services